INSIDE MLB

NEW YORK METS

Sam Rhodes

Go to www.av2books.com, and enter this book's unique code.

BOOK CODE

AVA57268

AV² by Weigl brings you media enhanced books that support active learning.

AV² provides enriched content that supplements and complements this book. Weigl's AV² books strive to create inspired learning and engage young minds in a total learning experience.

Your AV² Media Enhanced books come alive with...

Audio
Listen to sections of the book read aloud.

Key Words
Study vocabulary, and complete a matching word activity.

Video
Watch informative video clips.

Quizzes
Test your knowledge.

Embedded Weblinks
Gain additional information for research.

Slide Show
View images and captions, and prepare a presentation.

Try This!
Complete activities and hands-on experiments.

... and much, much more!

Published by AV² by Weigl
350 5th Avenue, 59th Floor
New York, NY 10118
Website: www.av2books.com

Library of Congress Control Number: 2017963670

ISBN 978-1-4896-7968-0 (hardcover)
ISBN 978-1-4896-7969-7 (softcover)
ISBN 978-1-4896-7970-3 (multi-user eBook)

Printed in the United States of America in Brainerd, Minnesota
1 2 3 4 5 6 7 8 9 0 22 21 20 19 18

012018
120817

Project Coordinator: John Willis   Designer: Nick Newton

Every reasonable effort has been made to trace ownership and to obtain permission to reprint copyright material. The publishers would be pleased to have any errors or omissions brought to their attention so that they may be corrected in subsequent printings.

The publisher acknowledges Getty Images, Alamy, Newscom, and iStock as its primary image suppliers for this title.

Contents

GO, METS!

The New York Mets are also known as the Amazin' Mets and the Miracle Mets. They are not one of the oldest teams in baseball, but they are one of the most popular. Through ups and downs, their fans support them. In more than 55 seasons as a Major League Baseball (MLB) team, they have become a New York **institution**.

Travis d'Arnaud scored one home run in 2013, the year he started with the Mets. He went on to hit 16 home runs during the 2017 season.

Joan Whitney Payson, the original owner of the Mets, was the third woman to own a MLB team.

Mets pitcher Jacob deGrom struck out almost 30 percent of the batters he faced in 2017. His season record earned him a nomination for the Cy Young Award, an annual award given to the best pitcher in each league.

Who Are the Mets?

Major League Baseball is actually two leagues, American and National, combined. Both leagues are made up of West, Central and East **divisions**. The Mets play in the National League (NL) East Division. After the regular season, the top team in each division, plus a wild card team from each league, goes to the playoffs, or postseason. The Mets have made nine playoff appearances.

Right fielder and first baseman Rusty Staub hit 75 home runs during his nine years with the New York Mets in the 1970s and 1980s.

WHERE THEY CAME FROM

The Mets joined the NL in 1962 with the Houston Astros as part of a two-team league **expansion**. When choosing a team name, owner Joan Whitney Payson rejected many options, including the Rebels, Skyliners, and Burros. She settled on the New York Mets. For their first two seasons, the Mets played home games on a field made for playing **polo**. Finally, in 1964, their new stadium opened.

In one of the last games of the 2017 season, the Mets beat the Phillies in the 11th inning, thanks to a three-run home run by Asdrúbal Cabrera.

Who They Play

Each team in the MLB plays 162 games in a season. The Mets play 76 of those games against other teams in their division. The other NL East teams are the Washington Nationals, the Miami Marlins, the Atlanta Braves, and the Philadelphia Phillies. The Mets have rivalries with the Phillies and Braves. They work hard and play their best, though, no matter which team they are up against.

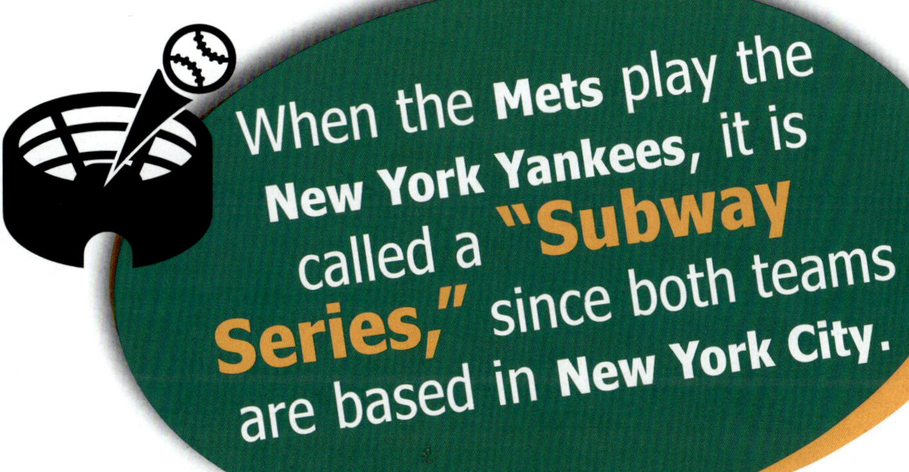

Where They Play

The Mets' first stadium was Shea Stadium, which opened in 1964. The team played there until 2008. In 2009, they moved to Citi Field, which was designed to make the fans more comfortable. It has wider seats and more **concession** stands. Citi Field can seat 41,800 fans at a time. There is even a Mets Hall of Fame and Museum inside the ballpark!

It took **three years** of construction and **12,540 tons** (11,376 metric tons) **of steel** to build **Citi Field**.

Citi Field has hosted more than 20 million fans since opening on April 13, 2009.

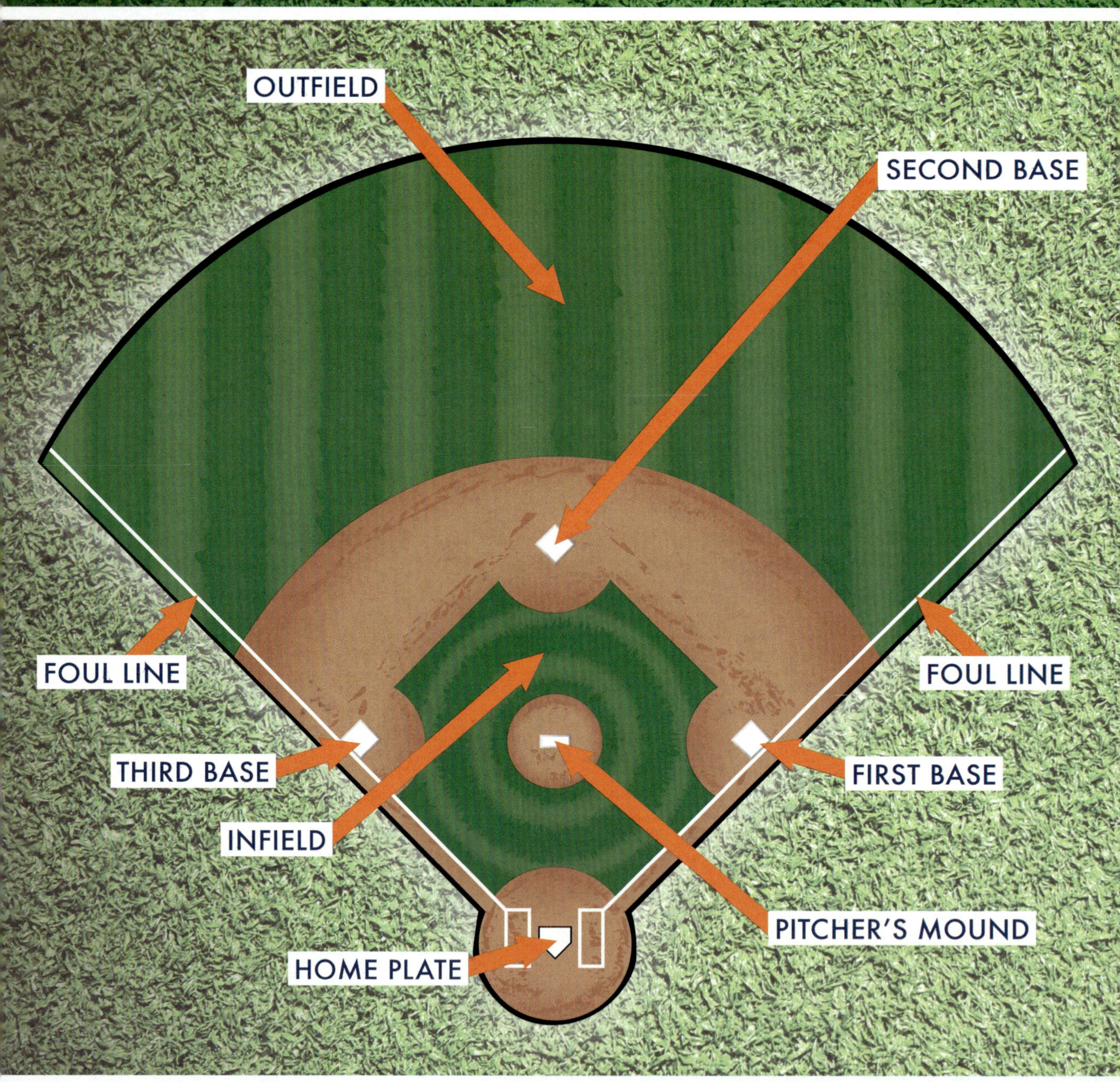
OUTFIELD
SECOND BASE
FOUL LINE
FOUL LINE
THIRD BASE
FIRST BASE
INFIELD
PITCHER'S MOUND
HOME PLATE

THE BASEBALL DIAMOND

Baseball games are played on a field called a diamond. Four bases form this diamond shape. The bases are 90 feet (27 meters) apart. The area around and between the bases is called the infield. At the center of the infield is the pitcher's mound. The grass area beyond the bases is called the outfield. White lines start at **home plate** and go toward the outfield. These are the foul lines. Baseballs hit outside these lines are out of play unless a fielder catches them. The outfield walls are about 300–450 feet (91–137 m) from home plate.

Big Days

The Mets have had some big wins over the years. Here are some of their finest seasons:

1969: *In their first year in the NL East, the Mets won their division. This was the first time in* ***franchise*** *history. The Mets' first World Series appearance ended in their first World Series victory. They trounced the Baltimore Orioles four games to one.*

1986: *The Amazin' Mets logged their best regular-season record ever, with 108 wins. The Mets faced the Boston Red Sox in the World Series. In Game 7, the Mets won the series with an 8–5 victory.*

2000: *The Mets finished the season second in their division. They made it into the playoffs as a wild card team. In an unlikely postseason run, the Mets advanced to the World Series. They lost to the New York Yankees, but stunned the world with their determination.*

During the 2000 NL Championship Series, the Mets won four of their five games against the St. Louis Cardinals. Game 5 was a complete shutout, with a final score of 7–0.

Despite the Mets' strong batting effort, with 6 home runs and 18 runs batted in (RBIs), and solid pitching, including 37 strikeouts, the team still fell to the Kansas City Royals during the 2015 World Series.

Tough Days

The Mets have also seen their share of hard times.

1962: *In their first MLB season, the Mets had a terrible year. They lost 120 games and only won 40. It was the worst record of all four new teams from the 1961 and 1962 expansions.*

1973: *The Mets fought to get to the top of their division. In the playoffs, they beat Cincinnati and went to the World Series for the second time. The Mets could not meet the high expectations, though, and fell to the Oakland Athletics in Game 7.*

2015: *The Mets were hoping for a third World Series championship in 2015. They had a great postseason. The Mets swept the Chicago Cubs with four straight wins in the NL Championship Series. Then, in the World Series, they were nearly swept themselves. They lost to the Kansas City Royals four games to one.*

Mr. Met stands tall at 6 feet, 10 inches (208 centimeters). He lists his weight as "top heavy."

MEET THE FANS

Mr. Met is the biggest Met fan ever. At least, he is the one with the biggest head. His enormous, smiling, baseball-shaped head can be spotted at all Mets home games. Mr. Met debuted on April 17, 1964. He was the first live-action mascot in the major leagues. In a 2016 poll, he was voted one of the most popular sports mascots in the country.

During his 12 seasons with the New York Mets, Tom Seaver won more than 60 percent of the games he pitched.

Mike Piazza, Catcher

Heroes Then...

The Mets franchise has had some spectacular players. Tom "Terrific" Seaver pitched for the Mets from 1967 to 1976. In 1969, on the way to the Mets' first World Series victory, Seaver led the NL with the most wins as a pitcher. Center fielder Lenny Dykstra walloped homers to help win the 1986 World Series for the Mets. Howard Johnson played shortstop with the Mets from 1985 to 1993. In 1991, he ranked first in the NL in home runs and RBIs. Mike Piazza joined the Mets in 1998. He was one of the best catchers in the NL and a powerful batter. He won four **Silver Slugger awards** in seven years with the team. Third baseman David Wright was an outstanding fielder. He won the **Gold Glove Award** twice. Wright also played for the NL **All-Star Game** team seven times between 2004 and 2016.

Heroes Now...

The Mets team today is full of incredible talent. Jacob deGrom is a Mets pitcher who won **Rookie** of the Year in 2014. He has ranked in the top 10 in earned run average and strikeouts in multiple seasons. Shortstop José Reyes has played for the Mets off and on since 2003. He has won numerous awards, including the NL title for best batting average in 2011. The Mets drafted left fielder Michael Conforto in 2015. He is a promising young player. Conforto went to the 2017 NL All-Star Game for the Mets. Left fielder Yoenis Céspedes is a veteran ballplayer who joined the Mets in 2015. Since then, he has won a Silver Slugger Award and proved himself to be an excellent fielder. Playing alongside Céspedes, center fielder Juan Lagares has been with the Mets since 2013. He won a Gold Glove Award for fielding in 2014.

Jacob deGrom, Pitcher

The present-day Mets are loaded with star players.

José Reyes, Shortstop

Michael Conforto, Left Fielder

GEARING UP

Baseball players all wear a team jersey and pants. They have to wear a team hat in the field and a helmet when batting. Take a look at Kevin Plawecki and Brandon Nimmo to see some other parts of a baseball player's uniform.

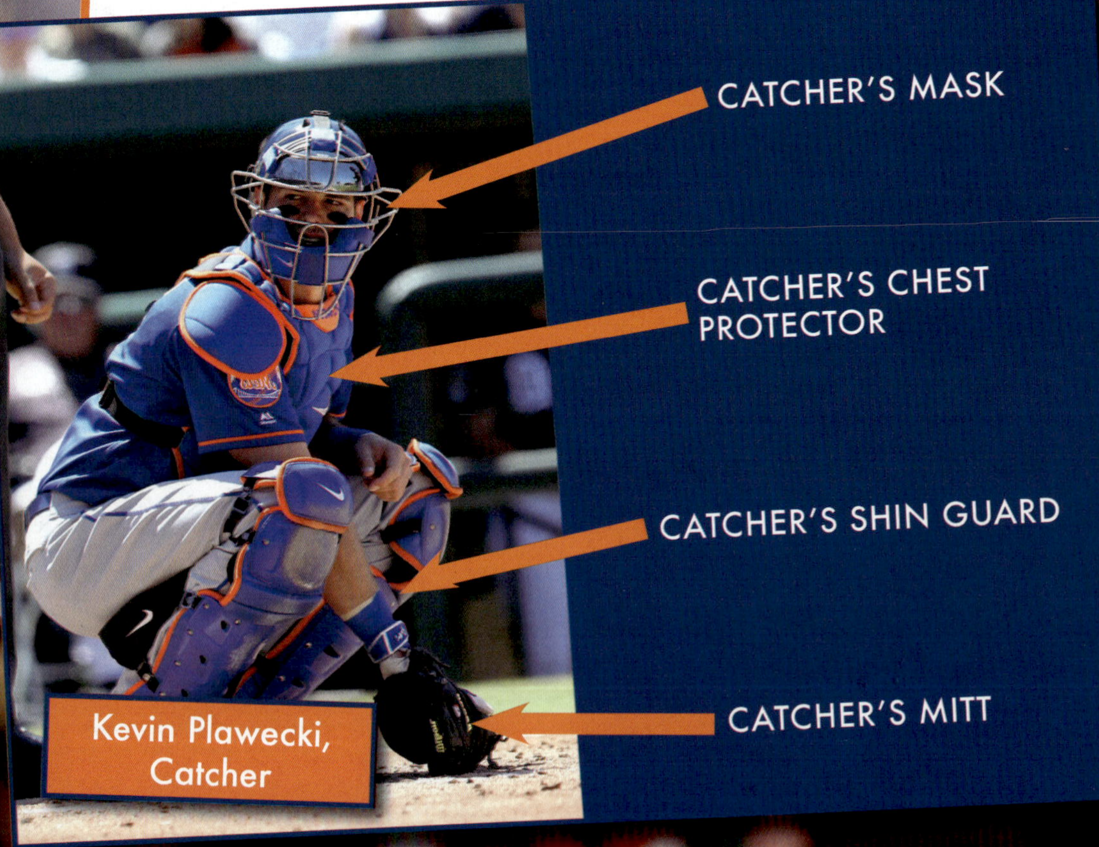

Kevin Plawecki, Catcher

BAT
BATTING HELMET
BATTING GLOVES
TEAM JERSEY
TEAM PANTS
Brandon Nimmo,
Outfielder
BASEBALL CLEATS

SPORTS STATS

Here are some all-time career records for the New York Mets. All of the stats are through the 2017 season.

A Major League baseball weighs about **5 ounces** (142 grams). It is **9 inches** (23 cm) around. A leather cover surrounds **hundreds** of feet of string. That string is wound around a small center of **rubber** and **cork**.

Home Runs

Darryl Strawberry, **252**

David Wright, **242**

Runs Batted In

David Wright, **970**

Darryl Strawberry, **733**

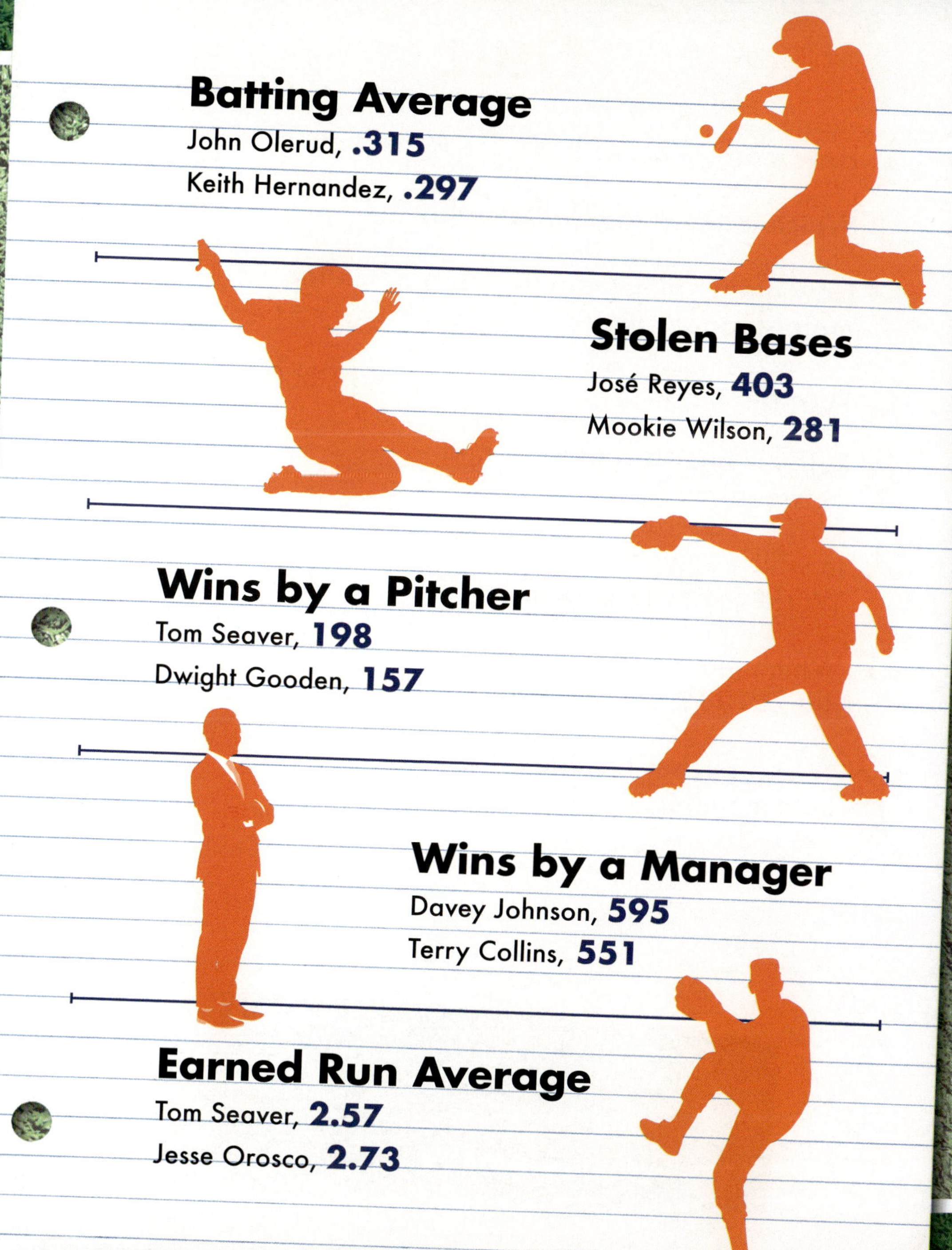

Batting Average

John Olerud, **.315**

Keith Hernandez, **.297**

Stolen Bases

José Reyes, **403**

Mookie Wilson, **281**

Wins by a Pitcher

Tom Seaver, **198**

Dwight Gooden, **157**

Wins by a Manager

Davey Johnson, **595**

Terry Collins, **551**

Earned Run Average

Tom Seaver, **2.57**

Jesse Orosco, **2.73**

Quiz

1 How many seasons have the Mets played?

2 Which league do the Mets play in?

3 How many games does each team in the major leagues play in a season?

4 How many years did it take to build Citi Field?

5 What is the area around and between the bases called?

6 In which year did the Mets have their first World Series appearance and victory?

7 Which team did the Mets face in the 2015 World Series?

8 Which pitcher has the most wins as a member of the Mets?

Answers

1. More than 55
2. The National League
3. 162
4. Three
5. The infield
6. 1969
7. The Kansas City Royals
8. Tom Seaver

Key Words

All-Star Game: an annual midseason game in which the best players from the AL and NL play against each other

concession: a place to sell something, such as food or drinks

divisions: groups of teams that form one part of a professional sports league

expansion: in baseball, the addition of new teams

franchise: a team that belongs to a professional sports league

Gold Glove Award: an annual award given to a player from each defensive position of each league

home plate: the base where a batter stands and where a runner must touch to score a run

institution: a custom with a long tradition

polo: a game played on horseback where players use mallets to hit a wooden ball into their opponent's goal

rookie: a sports player in his or her first year playing

Silver Slugger awards: annual awards given to a player from each offensive position of each league

Index

Log on to www.av2books.com

AV² by Weigl brings you media enhanced books that support active learning. Go to www.av2books.com, and enter the special code found on page 2 of this book. You will gain access to enriched and enhanced content that supplements and complements this book. Content includes video, audio, weblinks, quizzes, a slide show, and activities.

AV² Online Navigation

Audio
Listen to sections of the book read aloud.

Book Pages
AV² pages directly correspond to pages in the book.

Video
Watch informative video clips.

Embedded Weblinks
Gain additional information for research.

Key Words
Study vocabulary, and complete a matching word activity.

Try This!
Complete activities and hands-on experiments.

Quizzes
Test your knowledge.

Slide Show
View images and captions, and prepare a presentation.

AV² was built to bridge the gap between print and digital. We encourage you to tell us what you like and what you want to see in the future.

Sign up to be an AV² Ambassador at www.av2books.com/ambassador.

Due to the dynamic nature of the Internet, some of the URLs and activities provided as part of AV² by Weigl may have changed or ceased to exist. AV² by Weigl accepts no responsibility for any such changes. All media enhanced books are regularly monitored to update addresses and sites in a timely manner. Contact AV² by Weigl at 1-866-649-3445 or av2books@weigl.com with any questions, comments, or feedback.